Managing Your Online Reputation

Owning & Controlling your Brand

By Tammy Finch

Contents

Introduction: What is the Internet Saying About You?..7

Chapter 1: What You Need to Know About Your Online Reputation (and Why)................................11

Chapter 2: Discovering Your Online Reputation in 7 Easy Steps...21

Chapter 3: Establishing Your Online Reputation ...34

Chapter 4: Your Three-Step Process for Dealing With Online Reputation Problems..........................44

Chapter 5: Growing a Healthy Online Reputation..56

Chapter Six: Going Deep With Advanced Online Reputation Improvement Strategies 69

Chapter 7: Setting Good Social Media Policies for Your Business...79

Chapter 8: Common Online Reputation Management Mistakes..88

Chapter 9: Your Personal Online Reputation 106

Chapter 10: Some Parting Thoughts on Reputation Management...119

Copyright and disclaimer

Acknowledgements

I would like to take this space to thank a few people: my wonderful children, Ashley and Jamie who have always been my cheerleaders. They make being a mom a very easy job for me.

My husband, Chris, who is okay if I spend extra time working. He understands doing what you love is not work.

And finally, my family who think I am a lot smarter than I actually am.

About The Author

Thank you for taking the time to read my book! I'm Tammy Finch, a website designer and social media consultant and the founder of Web Services, Inc. in East Peoria, IL. In more than a dozen years in the web design and online marketing industry, I have had the opportunity to work with hundreds of clients, locally and nationally.

I currently manage several hundred websites and social profiles for my clients, and I'm a presenter on the topic of social media and online reputation management. Associations and business audiences around the country have turned to me for workshops on Facebook, Twitter, and LinkedIn, which I feel collectively represent one of the largest untapped opportunities for organizations of all sizes to find new members or customers, improve customer relationships, and even recruit new employees.

Beyond my keynotes and training sessions, I contribute to a number of business publications, both nationally and locally. I'm also available for customized social media consulting and training, and offer social media marketing packages through Web Services, Inc.

You can find out more about me, my presentations, and my services at www.webservicesinc.net.

Introduction: What is the Internet Saying About You?

Why do other people decide to do business with you and your company?

On the surface, that answer is probably easy. Maybe you have a good location, offer the best products, or can boast lower prices than any of your competitors. These are all great advantages to have.

And yet, they aren't enough. Millions of people purchase products and services every single day from companies that *don't* have the best selection, and sometimes pay higher prices to do so. At times, this might be a matter of habit or convenience. But, there is also another factor at play – one that determines who will win a new customer, recruit a talented employee, or earn more money much more often than we tend to realize.

That hidden factor is *reputation*. And in the digital age, reputation grows and spreads faster than ever, and can have an enormous impact on your bottom line.

In this book, I'm going to fill you in on the what if's, ups, and downs of online reputation management. I'm going to give you all the basics you need to know in order to run your company, including where your online reputation comes from, how it impacts your business and career, and what you can do to shape it.

Best of all, I'm going to give you all of this without any fluff, technical jargon, or extraneous material. I know you have other things to do and worry about, and I'm going to boil the essentials down into something you can read, understand, and use in a heartbeat.

Before we get into the details, though, let's make sure you understand who this book is written for, and who I am to be giving this advice in the first place.

I'll start by introducing myself. My name is Tammy Finch, and I'm the owner and president of Web Services, Inc. in Peoria, Illinois. I've been working in the web design and Internet marketing industry for more than two decades, specializing in the development of cost-effective campaigns for small businesses. In other words, I'm the kind of person you call when you need a great website and a way to find lots of new customers… and need all of that on a budget.

It won't surprise you to know that most of my time is spent working with, and thinking about, smaller companies. So, most of my advice is going to be geared toward small business owners, managers, and independent consultants. I'm going to assume that if you're reading this book you fall into one of those categories.

That isn't to say that executives from larger companies, nonprofits, or even governmental agencies can't learn from the coming chapters. If anything, these types of organizations have *more* to worry about when it comes to online reputation management. At the same time, however, they are likely to have big budgets and complex branding campaigns, not to mention consultants and social media strategists who are on call at all times.

Most of the men and women I deal with are either handling things on their own, or getting limited assistance from partners, employees, and vendors. This book is for them, and all of you who are in their same shoes. I'm going to give you some short-and-sweet advice about establishing and maintaining the right kind of image on the Internet so your business can thrive.

Does that sound good to you? If so, let's begin…

Chapter 1: What You Need to Know About Your Online Reputation (and Why)

Five or ten years ago, the term "online reputation management" was barely invented. Very few of us were talking about it, and most businesses were concerned with finding customers over the Internet, rather than worrying about what existing ones might or might not be saying about them.

But the growth and success of Internet marketing changed the way those processes worked. All of a sudden, customers weren't just finding websites and buying products or services... they were interested in researching companies *before* they scheduled a meeting or shared a credit card number. And the growth of social media made it easier for people to share real advice and reviews, positive or negative, in a way that hadn't been possible in the past.

In just a couple of years, the world's oldest and most powerful marketing tool – word-of-mouth advertising – was suddenly a "hot trend" that was moving along with a different name. People were still trading insight, impressions, and advice — they were just doing it online instead of discussing vendors and companies over a cup of coffee.

Through the course of this book, I'm going to share with you the basics of online reputation management. As we move from one topic in each chapter to the next, though, I want you to remember something very important: that what we are really talking about is word-of-mouth advertising being expanded, amplified, and enhanced by the Internet. It's about knowing and shaping the impressions that buyers, vendors, and employees have about you and your business, and understanding what they mean for the future of your business.

To make sure we get started on the right foot, let's begin by exploring what your online reputation is, in a more complete sense, and how it affects your company and career.

Where Does Your Online Reputation Come from?

As I've already mentioned, your online reputation is really just an extension of your *offline* reputation. It comes from the same sources (basically people who know you and have worked with you), but gets a much wider audience on the Internet.

To understand why this is, let's look at a very straightforward example. Suppose for a moment that you own a bakery. A customer comes in one morning and enjoys the best cinnamon roll they've ever had in their lives. Even better, the price is great, your staff is friendly, and the pastry looks like such a beautiful piece of art that they were almost afraid to eat it in the first place.

In the "old days," a.k.a. just a few years ago, this customer might have gone about their day, told one or two close friends about the great experience they had at your bakery, and then forgotten all about it. In fact, they might not have ever thought about your bakery or mentioned it again until they happened to drive by or were asked specifically about a good place to buy some sweets. The power of that word-of-mouth advertising would have been largely dependent on chance.

In the digital age, things get better. Now, that same customer might take to Facebook or Twitter and praise your bakery *while the experience is still fresh in their mind*. If you're lucky, they may even post pictures, or write a review on a website like Yelp.

This isn't *really* any different than what would've happened with plain old word-of-mouth advertising, but there are three big differences. The first is that their recommendation of your bakery can reach a much larger audience through social media than it would have in casual conversation. So, that endorsement goes a lot farther.

The second is that the recommendation is likely to be more specific. That's partly because the experience will still be fresh in the customer's mind (meaning they are less likely to forget your name, location, etc.), but it also has to do with the proliferation of smart phones. It's one thing for a friend or colleague to *hear* that cinnamon roll was great; it's another thing entirely for them to be able to *see* it with their own eyes.

The third difference, though, is the one that's really important: that recommendation stays online indefinitely. So, while most of the people in your customer's contact list will see their endorsement almost immediately, it will stay on the Internet for others – including those looking for bakeries and cinnamon rolls – to find for months and years to come. They may even be indexed by Google, so that anyone looking for businesses like yours sees a customer singing your praises in their search results.

It's not hard to see how that dynamic could do wonders for your sales. Now, imagine what would happen if there were dozens of positive reviews floating around!

From this straightforward example, you can start to understand where it is your online reputation is built from. It's made up of lots of impressions, of course, and they can come from many, many different places. Webpages, social media posts, online reviews, video clips, and even blogs can all contribute to the way you and your business are perceived on the Internet.

One important caveat here is to note that, while some of your online reputation will stem from content *you* create, the majority can be traced back to other people. To put it more plainly, you can try to set your online reputation in the right direction, but it's hard to control. You have to encourage customers, employees, and others to say the right things about you online. That's a topic and idea we will return to throughout the short book.

Before we get into how you can create and encourage those impressions, though, let's take a quick look at the different ways your online reputation can affect your business, and even your career…

How Your Online Reputation Affects Your Business

"All of this sounds great," you might be thinking, "but are things like Internet reviews and social posting *really* going to affect my bottom line?" I can assure you that they will. In fact, they are already, regardless of whether you're aware of it or not.

The difference won't just be in your ability to attract new customers, either. Although a change in your online reputation will likely be felt in your sales receipts *first*, there are several parts of your company that will be impacted if your online reputation is improved or diminished.

For example, new buyers who come to you after reading great things about your business online are more likely to place orders quickly, and are less prone to haggling over prices. So, your reputation affects not only your ability to win the customer, but also what kind of profit margin you can get from their order.

To look at things from another perspective, businesses with great reputations can attract talented and driven employees. By contrast, businesses with bad reputations are the ones that no one wants to work for. So, we can confidently say that reputation management will affect your recruiting efforts in a profound way — and that, in turn, can have a spillover effect to the rest of your business.

In some businesses, vendors are as important as employees. But, if you're constantly being trashed over the

Internet, it's a good bet that reputable professionals, or other businesses in good standing, aren't going to be lining up to work with you. Or if they are, they are going to adjust their terms because of the perceived risk.

And of course, you can't have a strong brand without a good reputation, since the two go hand-in-hand. That means that a good online reputation makes all of your marketing more effective, and a bad online reputation undercuts your efforts to get attention or raise public awareness about your organization.

We'll look at more ways that your reputation affects your company in a bottom line sense throughout the coming chapters. However, the critical point to note here is that having a good online reputation isn't just about posting a few blogs or hoping people will like you – it's something that can make or break your business on several levels over the course of time.

The Personal Consequences of Reputation Management

Even though this book is primarily directed at small businesses, it's worth mentioning that reputation management affects individuals, too. In some companies, the owner essentially is the business, making those personal impressions all the more crucial.

The easiest way to understand reputation management from a personal point of view is to think of things from a job-search perspective. Businesses of all sizes routinely lookup potential employees on Google, social media accounts, and elsewhere, to see what they've been up to. The resulting information can easily determine whether an applicant will be taken seriously or not.

To better illustrate the issue, let me share an example from my own life. Many years ago, I invested in a small rental house in a town not far from my home. Over the years, I've had several different relatives rented for me. When I ran out of cousins, nieces, and nephews looking for a place to stay, I finally had to put an ad on Craigslist.

Because I know potential tenants *always* put their best foot forward when trying to impress a new employer or landlord, one of the first things I do after receiving a rental application is check the person's profile on Facebook. It's a cheap and easy way of looking into their background and making sure that what they've told me matches up with reality.

The first person who applied to live in my home had left his Facebook page public, so I could see all of his posts. On the day I checked, it seemed as if he'd had too many Jägermeister the night before and was calling in to work. It took somewhere around three seconds for my brain to practically scream "next!"

My second applicant was a young woman moving from Wisconsin who seemed really sweet on the phone. When I went to check her Facebook page, however, I got a slightly different impression. Her cover photo was a picture of cannabis, with the phrase "F*ck school, smoke weed!" written inside. I couldn't view any more than that within her profile, but would I really need to? Needless to say, I didn't want her smoking pot in my house.

On my third try I had better luck. My applicant had a normal -looking profile, with a few pictures of his truck, his family, and his love of fishing and online gaming. We signed the lease, and he's been a great tenant. He pays his rent on time every month, and last I heard he met a nice girl at his new job in town.

I'm not exactly a detective, and my standards for potential tenants are pretty basic. So, if I could easily disqualify two people from renting from me within a few seconds of a social media search, imagine how a bigger employer – or someone with more at stake – is going to look at the material you post online… or the material that's being posted about you.

While some employers will certainly look the other way on party pics and not-suitable-for-work humor, these can easily serve as "red flags" that convince recruiters to direct their attention elsewhere. The same goes for messages that contain religious or political content that might indicate future problems in the workplace.

Even after you've gotten a job, your online reputation can affect your ability to be promoted, go back to school, or take other steps forward professionally.

And finally, I would be remiss if I didn't point out that your online reputation can definitely have an influence on your social relationships, as well. I'm not going to get into the issues of online bullying, cyber stalking, or Internet dating here, because they are beyond the scope of the topic I'm getting at. Just know that things posted by or about you to any kind of app, webpage, or social media account are always at risk of being seen by people they weren't intended for. This is *especially* true for items that could be sensitive or embarrassing.

How Well do You Know Your Online Reputation?

Now that we have briefly covered what your online reputation is and the many ways it can affect your business and/or personal life, it's time to figure out what yours is actually like right now so you can know what you're dealing with (and what potential customers, vendors, or employers are seeing when they look you up). That's the exact topic we are going to cover in the next chapter…

Chapter 2: Discovering Your Online Reputation in 7 Easy Steps

---

As you probably realize by now, your online reputation is more than just a few reviews or social updates… and it can have a tremendous effect on your profitability. For that reason, enhancing yours should be a big priority.

Before you can improve your online reputation, you have to know what others are saying about you in the first place. That probably seems like a pretty straightforward notion, but you'd be surprised at how many new clients I deal with who have literally *no idea* of the things that have been posted about them all over the web.

In this chapter, I'm going to walk you through a quick, seven-step process you can follow to get a sense of what your online reputation is like. Later, we'll see what you can do to improve your profile, deal with any problem areas, and start to shape the impressions that customers, vendors, and employees have about you and your business.

Let's start with the best ways to see what all of these groups are finding right now…

Step #1: Google Yourself

If you haven't ever googled your own name to see what comes up, or haven't done so recently, this is a great first step to take towards checking out your online reputation. That's because Google is not only the web's top clearinghouse for information coming from thousands of different sources, but it's also the first step anyone who's thinking of working with you is likely to take.

It's likely that you already check out potential customers, vendors, and employees by looking them up on Google (and if you don't you should start doing so today). Why not see what the world's most popular search engine is telling people about you?

A quick Google search of your own name will give you a good overview of your online reputation, if you have one. But rather than simply browsing the available material and forming a few quick impressions, I encourage you to go a bit deeper and follow a few simple guidelines.

First, go beyond the initial page or two of results. Although a lot of customers and colleagues might not take this step, it's important because some important results might be buried farther down the listings.

Next, try different variations of your name, including things like your middle name, the city where you live, your occupation, and so on. If you have a fairly common name, there might be dozens of different people who show up in the results. That can be good and bad (more on that later), but for now you want to see what kind of information comes up about you specifically.

Make a note of anything that seems especially good or bad. In fact, it's a good idea to bookmark these pages so you can return to them later.

And finally, remember to repeat this exercise again on a regular basis. Simply Googling your own name isn't going to tell you all you need to know about your online reputation, but it's a quick and easy first step, and a way to find out what potential customers might be seeing about you without spending hours digging into your reputation online.

Step #2: Do the Same for Your Business

Once you have a good idea of what's been posted about you on Google, it's time to do the same thing for your company or organization. I often find that a lot of business owners and managers know a great deal about what's been posted about them personally, but aren't as sure what customers are saying about the company as a whole.

The same rules from the first step apply here. You'll want to dig deeply into the search results, note anything that seems like a positive or negative, and revisit this exercise again over time.

One particular thing to note at this stage, however, is that a lot of the impressions that people have about your business might have nothing to do with you. Perhaps you bought the company from someone else, have had employees or contractors who did work under your name, or even deal with customers who confuse you with one of your competitors.

In each of these cases, the material that's being posted online – even if it isn't current or factual – still impacts you. So don't dismiss something you read out of hand because you think it's not relevant. To someone who's considering spending money with your business, every impression counts.

Step #3: Check Online Reviews

There are a lot of different places people can post reviews about your business and the interactions they've had with you. The obvious choices are Yelp and social media platforms like Facebook or Google +, but there are also online retailers, industry websites, local business directories, and even websites where employees and contractors rate the organizations they work with.

Starting with the websites that seem like obvious choices to you (for instance, TripAdvisor if you deal with tourists, or CNET if you sell technology products) make a list of all the places where customers have (or can) share feedback about your company. Make note of whether any reviews are present, how current they are, and what kinds of impressions those reviews give.

Go as deeply as you can with this search, and try to leave no stone unturned. As I mentioned before, there may be some material you think is irrelevant, but you would be surprised at how easily some small bit of feedback can affect your reputation.

For example, if a disgruntled intern once posted something negative about your company or attitude, that might seem unlikely to have any effect on future sales. But it all factors into the overall picture that buyers, vendors, and future employees get when researching you. And, it doesn't take much to scare somebody who's skeptical away.

Of course, the opposite is also true, and even small bits of positive feedback – especially in the form of customer reviews – can go a long way towards enhancing your credibility.

Step #4: Review Your Own Social Posts

Reviewing your own social activity is a simple step, but it's one that a lot of business owners never take. After all, you already *know* what you've said on Facebook, Twitter, and elsewhere… right?

The answer isn't as straightforward as you might think. For one thing, it's easy to forget about posts made in the past. Perhaps your views or attitude on a certain subject have changed since you originally shared a thought or idea.

Also, even if you know what you've said on social media sites, how positive are you that you know what friends and relatives have posted about you? Even if you're conscientious about the way you present yourself online, could someone else have shared a photo or idea that doesn't necessarily present you in the best light?

The biggest reason to review your own social history, however, has to do with the fact that not everyone is going to share your opinions or read your ideas in the way they were intended. This brings us into a bit of a gray area when it comes to your online reputation, but one that is nonetheless very important.

It's not at all unusual for men and women of all ages to add (or share) comments, updates, and pictures that could be considered off-color, politically-divisive, or inflammatory to someone else with different religious or moral viewpoints. I'm not going to tell you that you can't have and express your personality online – that is certainly your right as an individual – but I *am* going to tell you that these types of posts can very easily hurt your business.

If you like to share things about your religion or politics, for example, know that those kinds of posts are going to bring some customers closer and push others farther away. Is it worth it for you to make sure everyone knows your views about the upcoming election, if it causes half of your potential clients to take their business elsewhere? I can't make that decision for you, but it's something to think about.

I know a gentleman who owns a local business in central Illinois. If you are a polite person, which he certainly isn't, you could probably say that he's "passionate" about his political views. So passionate, in fact, that he started sharing them through his business accounts on LinkedIn and Facebook.

The interesting thing about these posts was that they generated a ton of engagement. People were certainly responding to what he had to say. Unfortunately, a lot of the feedback was extraordinarily negative, and the discussions often took on a heated tone.

I was so intrigued by his approach to social media that I invited him to an event where I was speaking. Not long after, he contacted me for a free consultation.

During that meeting, I gave him some good advice about keeping his business post business topics, and not strain into areas of sports, religion, and politics that tended to be divisive. He countered this notion, bragging that he had many more followers than he would have if he had simply stuck to promoting his business. I had to concede that he was right, but what did it matter? The people coming to his business pages weren't fans, they were others who are looking to pick a fight. In fact, he spent a lot of time every day simply cleaning up profanity and deleting posts from his social profiles.

In the end, I explained that the types of followers he was attracting with his views were not helping his business. If anything, they were probably alienating his real clients and prospects. My suggestion to him was the same one I give to anyone using their social accounts to promote controversial personal agendas: remember your goal and stick to the script. Starting arguments online isn't going to do anything positive.

Whatever you share about yourself, and your personal beliefs, has to be a conscious choice. My own suggestion might be to keep things that are controversial on your personal accounts, at the very least, and to save your business profiles for professional thoughts and messages. But since anything you post online can be found by buyers and the public at large, you're going to have to decide where to draw the line.

As one last thought on reviewing your own social posts, pay attention to things like grammar and typos. People are obviously a lot more forgiving on social media than they would be in a book or newspaper, but it's easy to hurt your own credibility if others get the sense that you can't express yourself clearly enough to be taken seriously.

Step #5: Start a News Feed

One of the best features of the web is that it's in constant motion. Things like news, forecasts, and even opinions can be updated in real time. The downside to all that activity, however, is that it makes it more difficult to keep a close eye on your online reputation. After all, someone could add a new thought or review about your business hours, or even minutes, after you've gone through this entire process.

The best way to keep up with everything that's going on around you is by setting up a newsfeed. There are number of ways to do this (including a free tool offered by Google itself) that will alert you anytime something new shows up around a predefined set of keywords or search terms.

I strongly suggest you start a newsfeed that incorporates, at a minimum, your name, your company's name, and your industry with the geographic location (for instance, "Peoria accountants"). You might also include employee names, competitor names, and anything else that you feel is strongly relevant to what you do. You can always ignore items that don't affect you, or your online reputation, but it's better to have slightly too much information than it is to have too little.

Step #6: Use Social Listening Tools

While a newsfeed will keep you alerted to big items like announcements, press releases, and new webpages, you also want to keep an ear to the ground on social media sites like Facebook and Twitter. That's where social listening tools come in.

Like newsfeeds, these are incredibly simple to set up, and can help you follow conversations about your company, industry, or other relevant topic. You can sort items by keyword, author, or hashtag, but the exact configuration isn't important. What matters is that you'll know whether someone is referencing you or your business on any major social media site.

Social listening tools are valuable for monitoring your online reputation, of course, but they can also help you to address questions or resolve customer concerns so that you deal with problems before they actually become problems. As we'll see in a later chapter, being proactive with customer care is one of the best ways to establish and nurture a strong online reputation. Social listening makes that a much more straightforward task.

Step #7: Check Out Employees, Associates, and Imposters

Just as each business owner has to decide how much of their "personality" to share on social accounts, they also have to decide how closely they want to monitor employees, vendors, and other people associated with their companies. Certainly, there are lines of privacy that are easy to cross, and micromanaging the people who work for you on social platforms can easily backfire.

Even with that caveat out of the way, there's no denying the fact that you should have some idea of what your colleagues and employees are up to online. After all, they aren't just in close contact with your customers, but they're the ones who are most likely to say good or bad things about your business. This doesn't mean you should stalk everyone who works for you online, just that you shouldn't be oblivious to the fact if they are slandering you or sharing company secrets.

We will examine the right and wrong ways to set a social media policy for your business in just a bit. For now, just know that anyone who is associated with you is factoring into your online reputation. For that reason, it makes sense to at least know what's going on in the background.

One final word needs to be said in this section, and it concerns online "imposters." In this context, I'm not talking about people who are impersonating you directly – although you should certainly take action if that's the case – but people who might have very similar names, or business names, to your own. The closer they are to you, in geography or type of business, the more likely it is that buyers are going to get the wrong idea.

For example, if there is a business one town over that has a very similar name to the one you own, and they have a terrible reputation for customer satisfaction, it's very likely that prospects will occasionally confuse your company with theirs. We'll look at some things you can do to address these kinds of issues, but knowing about them is the most important first step.

Chapter 3: Establishing Your Online Reputation

In the last chapter, I walked you through the process of discovering your current online reputation. But what if there's nothing to be found?

While having no online reputation isn't a terrible thing, because it's easy to fix, it isn't exactly great news, either. That's because having nothing posted about you online is nearly as bad as having negative reviews and impressions, at least in the minds of potential customers. After all, what does it say to them if you seem to be nonexistent on the web?

At best, it signals that your business isn't well-known and is difficult to find. That could undercut your credibility, especially if you're trying to promote your company as one with great products, a strong track record, or a habit of delivering top-tier service. It only stands to reason that, if any of those things are true, they would be easy to back up with real information from verified customers.

Another problem with having little or no online reputation is one I've already alluded to: that it becomes easy for potential customers, and the public at large, to confuse your business with other companies. When that happens, someone else's poor online reputation can hurt your sales. Or someone who intends to buy from you (because they were referred to you, for example) could end up purchasing from a competitor simply because they were easier to find.

The bottom line is that your online reputation can't help you grow and succeed if you don't have one in the first place. So let's take a look at some quick and easy steps you can follow to establish a presence and get people saying the right kinds of things about your company...

Search Optimize Your Business Website

In a perfect world, the information that potential customers and vendors would get about your business would come directly from you. That's why one of the best things you can do to improve your online reputation is to search optimize your business website.

Given that there is a virtually endless number of books and seminars on the topic of SEO, you're probably already at least somewhat familiar with the way it works. And if you aren't, it's definitely worth getting some professional help from an experienced web design team who can assist you in this area.

In the most basic sense, however, search engine optimization works like this: you add targeted search phrases to the most visible parts of your website (like headlines, page titles, etc.) so that Google and the other search engines can "understand" what your website is about. That, in turn, makes it easier for people who are searching for your business – or a company like yours – to find on the web.

Again, SEO is a very big topic. I could fill the rest of this book with search marketing details and barely scratch the surface. The point I want to make here is that the content on your website is *completely under your control.* By making it more visible, you ensure that one of the top two or three search results for your business is a very positive one, so long as your website is professionally-designed and set up in a way that will impress potential buyers.

Be Visible on Industry Websites and Local Business Directories

A moment ago I mentioned that search optimizing your website might gain you one of the top few positions in the search results when customers go looking for you or your company by name. You might be wondering why your website wouldn't be the *first* result for someone searching for your particular business.

In some cases it might be, especially if you are well known and your website is extensive. In other situations, however, there are likely to be other websites that Google "trusts" for information about your business more than your own pages. Profiles of your company on industry websites and local business directories, in particular, can effectively crowd you out of the top spots.

There is a simple reason for this: actual searchers like to find independent, verifiable information about a company they are thinking about doing business with. Google's engineers have noticed this and placed a priority on these types of search results.

Knowing that, one of the first things you need to do to establish your online reputation is to ensure that you have profiles on industry websites and local business directories, and that those profiles are complete and correct. In other words, things like website information, phone numbers, and mailing addresses should all be checked and double-checked. Photos should be added or improved when necessary.

Sometimes, administrators will create pages for businesses on their own to make a directory or industry resource more valuable. But, the listings they create could be based on outdated information. Given that they might appear at the top of a potential customer's search results – and thus have a big effect on your online reputation – you need to ensure that people can find you on these websites, and that the information listed is current and correct.

Use Complete Profiles on All the Major Social Media Sites

Like business directories, social media profiles can be ranked heavily into search engine results. In addition, many potential customers, partners, and employees will look for information about you or your business on social media first, meaning that profiles on Facebook, Google +, and especially LinkedIn can all be very important to your online reputation.

That's all very easy to understand, and yet there are lots of businesses – and business owners – who never take the time to set up profiles on Twitter, Pinterest, or other social media websites that they don't personally use on a regular basis. Make sure you don't duplicate that mistake. Don't just set up profiles, but complete them so there's no mistaking who you are and what you do.

What does a "complete" profile look like? That will change from one social platform to the next, of course, but you should include photos of your team and products (professional ones if you have them), links to your website, current contact information, and if possible, links to endorsements from satisfied customers. It also helps if you have at least a few posts that relate to your business and/or geographic area.

It doesn't take much work to set up complete profiles on the major social media sites, but doing so allows customers to research you, ask questions directly, and most importantly to add their own impressions and content (which will grow your online profile over time). So make it a priority to establish a broad social presence immediately.

Be Active on Social Media

While setting up different social profiles is a good first step, you'll need to have some regular activity on them if you want potential customers to actually notice.

Note that I'm *not* telling you that you have to spend every minute – or even every day – on social media. What I *am* saying is that a profile with no activity at all can actually hurt your online reputation because it suggests that nothing is going on with your business.

Maintaining a little bit of social activity doesn't have to take nearly as much time and effort as you might think. If you have a few profiles that are popular with your customers, and that you enjoy using, you might log-in for a few minutes a day to add a thought or respond to questions and inquiries. For other social media profiles that aren't as important to you and your business, a few minutes a week might suffice.

Being active on your social profiles tells potential contacts that you're "open for business," and invites them to engage with you. The more that happens, the more you are encouraging others to say something positive about their dealings with you, or to share something you've posted with their own contacts. That, over time, can go a long way towards boosting your online reputation.

Ask Satisfied Customers for Reviews

In a perfect world, you would have up-to-date profiles for your business on industry websites, local business directories, and social media platforms that would attract attention and reviews all on their own. In reality, though, you might need to get the ball rolling yourself.

For whatever reason, people are more likely to leave reviews and feedback after others have already done so. What's more, they are much more likely to say positive things about your business if other positive things have already been written. That's why a few good testimonials can snowball into a positive online reputation that helps you find more sales and opportunities. Or, for that matter, why a bit of negative feedback can push momentum in the wrong direction.

The big takeaway here is that your first few reviews and testimonials are crucial, and they might be difficult to get from new customers. So, why not make things easier and get them from existing buyers who already know you and like your work or products?

Paying for reviews, or soliciting them too heavily, can backfire as a reputation management strategy, and that's something we'll explore shortly. There's nothing disingenuous, however, about asking people you work with all the time – your biggest fans and supporters – to say good things about you online. Most will be happy to do it, especially if they know how much it means to your business.

So make a list of your dozen best customers and see if they might be willing to provide some kind words (or better yet, a testimonial with their name and picture) that can be posted on the web. Not only will these reviews help your online reputation immediately, but they could be just what you need to convince *other* satisfied buyers to come forward and add their compliments, too.

Make It Easy to Grow Your Online Reputation

Every business owner wants to have a positive online reputation, but many never take the simple-but-essential beginning steps to establish one in the first place.

Hoping that you'll become more visible online, and that customers will start to say good things about you out of nowhere, is a strategy that's based on hope, not effort. What's far more likely is that your business will get lost in the mix, and that others will contribute information that is either incorrect or out of date.

At a certain point, your online reputation *has* to grow out of the ideas that other people share about you and your business. Some of the factors will always be out of your control. You can set the tone, however, by taking control of the process early on in making sure that what's posted about your business on the most visible websites is correct, and that the people who have the best things to say about your business are being heard.

Chapter 4: Your Three-Step Process for Dealing With Online Reputation Problems

---

Most of us have had the experience, either as a child playing outside or an adult working in a garden, of lifting a stone off the ground and being at least a little bit surprised (and maybe a tiny bit horrified) of what we find underneath. Occasionally, turning over a stone yields all kinds of unexpected and unwanted insights into the giant world of insects and spiders that was hidden blissfully from view just a few moments ago.

Looking into your online reputation can be a little bit like that.

In the last chapter, I explained what you can do if you find that you have no online reputation to speak of. But what happens when you start digging and find things you really don't like? What if there are some issues with your reputation that are troublesome, or even serious threats to the future of your business?

We're going to look at exactly that in this chapter. The first step, though, is to stay calm. Regardless of how tough things look – or what kind of reviews and impressions you might be fighting – know that you're better off facing the problem head-on than you are pretending it doesn't exist. After all, if you continue to ignore your online reputation, who's to say it won't deter even more buyers in the future? And, as we'll see shortly, fixing a damaged online reputation isn't nearly as impossible as it might seem at first glance.

In fact, most issues can be cleared up by following three simple steps...

Step One: Fix the Problem

If you have negative online reviews and feedback, there's probably a good reason. Most business owners don't want to hear this, or even think about it, but the bad news that's posted about them online is often (but not always) the result of bad service that's been provided offline.

Knowing that, the first thing you can do to fix your online reputation – and the most important step – is to *correct the problem in your business that led to the bad review or feedback*. If buyers are consistently saying that your prices are too high, see if there are ways you can lower them or add more value. If customers complain that your cashiers are rude, then replace them, or give them rewards based on secret shopper experiences.

This isn't just good business sense, it's also a way to stop the bleeding. After all, if lots of people are giving your company poor marks because of an identifiable issue, then they are likely to continue doing so in the future until things change.

For issues that are more personal or situational, you'll want to take a different approach, but one that is still based on solving the problem. For example, suppose a bad online review was written by a customer who had a poor experience with your company. In this situation, the first impulse a lot of business owners have will be to contest the review, or write a scathing reply. That's a big mistake, because it only draws more attention to the issue, and makes you seem petty, vindictive, or worse.

So, instead of lashing out, I suggest you take steps, privately, to see if you can resolve the situation and make the customer happy again. Perhaps you can issue a coupon or refund. Maybe you can convince them to come and give you another try "on the house." Whatever it is, see if you can work the problem out in a way that satisfies everyone.

This is an important step because it is likely to stop the disgruntled customer from bad-mouthing you any further. In fact, it may even convince them to retract their previous review and submit something new… but if, and only if, they feel like you're being genuine.

I've seen these kinds of win-win outcomes occur dozens of times. One in particular comes to mind. A longtime client of mine – the president of a CPA firm in Chicago – called me in a panic after finding a complaint on Google about one of his employees. His firm had always been focused on customer service; if it wasn't for the personal attention they gave, they wouldn't have been able to compete with the bigger accounting companies around the city.

After talking with him for a while on the phone, I suggested he print out a copy of the review and speak to his employee to get her side of the story. It didn't take long for my client to find out that every single word was true. His employee *had* been rude to the customer, and was late to several meetings on top of that. Because there had been ongoing issues with this particular person, he had to let her go.

That in itself would have been a good first step for the reason I gave you before: it would have stopped the bleeding (in this case, more bad reviews stemming from poor experiences with this employee). But my client went even further. After things had settled down, he took the client in question to lunch and actually thanked her for the review, since it opened his eyes to a serious problem. Not only was he able to save the account, but the client actually wrote a follow-up review and testimonial that was so positive, he is still using them on his website today.

Listening to the feedback – and *especially* the bad feedback – that buyers give you is important. Besides placating a customer who might be slamming you all over the Internet, it also gives you a chance to hear their complaints more fully. That might be difficult, and you might not always agree, but remember that there might be five or ten other people who have the same complaint about your business but have never voiced it. What do you have to lose by hearing them out?

Regardless of how it's done, and what the specific circumstances are, fixing any problems with your service or business model is an important step towards cleaning up your online reputation. Otherwise, you'll always have bad reviews that stick out like sore thumbs, and they'll probably keep adding up over time.

Step Two: Explain Your Case and Fight Incorrect Information

More often than not, simply being responsive to repeated pieces of customer feedback and getting in touch with unsatisfied buyers directly is enough to remove any black marks in your online reputation. But when that doesn't do the trick, you might want to go on the offensive.

There are really three ways to go about this, but they all have the same goal: removing a prominent piece of bad feedback from the Internet. That's no easy task – we all know that what goes online tends to stay there forever – but it's not impossible.

The first method is to simply contact the individual involved on your own and ask them to remove the information themselves. This can be particularly effective if you've taken my advice in the earlier section and dealt with the problem in a private way already. Simply mentioning that you'd appreciate it if they would reconsider their position, based on the fact that you've done all that you can to make them happy, might be enough to get them to remove what they've posted (and possibly replace it with something better).

If that's not possible, you can follow the second tactic, which is to explain your side of the story. Although bad online reviews and impressions can be very harmful to your business, today's buyers are savvy. They know just as well as you do that not everyone can be pleased, and that some customers are going to be dissatisfied for rational reasons. So, telling your side of the story and letting readers know what happened from your perspective can help take some of the sting away from some bad feedback.

It's important to note at this point that your response should be calm and professional. The last thing you want to do is get involved in a mud-slinging contest with the customer, even if you feel justified. Doing so only hurts your online reputation further, and discourages prospects from wanting to do business with you (in case things don't work out and they find themselves on the receiving end of a rant). Keep things clean, upbeat, and focused on the situation at hand. Just emphasize that you did your best, and that the particular customer in question just couldn't be satisfied.

If you don't think explaining the situation will help, you can take the third option, which is to contest the review and ask that it be removed by the service that's hosting it (Facebook, Yelp, etc.).

In most cases, you'll be facing long odds to get a post or review by a former customer or employee taken off-line. After all, if every business had nothing but positive feedback, review sites wouldn't have any value at all. However, if you can show that the review is fraudulent, incorrect, or otherwise misleading (for instance, if it obviously applies to a different business nearby) then you might be able to convince a moderator to take it away.

As a short side note, the recent explosion in fraudulent online reviews is yet another reason to pay close attention to your online reputation and monitor it regularly. While you would probably never stoop to the level of having people post fake reviews of other businesses, your competitors might not be quite as ethical.

What do you do if none of these solutions works? In very extreme cases, you could seek legal action against the reviewer or review site, but the best answer is usually just to leave things be. Buyers already know that every business in the world is going to get negative feedback at some point or another. A handful of bad reviews, or subpar experiences, aren't going to hurt you if there are lots of other positive impressions to be found.

If you doubt this, visit Amazon.com and check out a few of the best-selling books or movies being offered. You'll find that the most popular titles have dozens, or even hundreds, of customer views (remember what I said earlier: once you have a few reviews, more will start to show up on their own). Even though the majority will be positive for these well-received works, there will inevitably be a handful of people who don't just hate the book or movie, but are very vocal and specific about their complaints.

That doesn't stop them from being best-sellers, and a few unhappy customers won't prevent other people from trying your business. Do what you can to clean out bad reviews, but don't dwell on them forever.

Step Three: Share the Good News

If you ask ten of your friends about a new restaurant in town, and nine of them like it, what is your overall impression? Are you excited to make a reservation, or worried about the one friend who didn't enjoy his meal?

This is a point I've returned to a couple of times because it's so critical: it's difficult to have a flawless online reputation, because people are so unpredictable, but being merely "great" is good enough. In fact, it might actually be better.

Here's why: when people see nothing but great reviews about your business, they get suspicious.

Having five really good reviews is helpful, but if there are dozens, and all five star ratings, then prospects may begin to wonder whether you or your marketing team are making them up yourselves.

Luckily or unluckily, that's not likely to happen naturally over time anyway. So, the key is to encourage happy buyers to let others know about their experiences. That way, the overall trend is always positive, your reviews are coming from real people, and any negative feedback is going to seem like an outlier – the exception that proves the rule.

Over time, getting lots of positive reviews for your business is more important to your online reputation than removing bad reviews is. The good news will more than make up for the bad.

I'll close this chapter with another first-hand example. One of my good clients is the owner and operator of an excellent catering company. Just a few months ago, he called me and said, "Tammy, business has really dropped off in the past six months. I normally don't have to do any advertising, but I'm starting to look into television commercials because I'm feeling panicked. Calls about new business have really dropped off significantly."

I told the client I'd look for an explanation and get back to him. Finding the root cause of his trouble only took a few minutes. A quick search for his business name revealed a handful of incredibly negative reviews on both Google and Yelp.

When I called the client back, we discussed the reviews in detail. He immediately knew exactly who had left them. It seems that these particular individuals were very unreasonable, first at the event that he catered, and then later online in leaving their reviews.

The food that he had given them was hot, delicious, and served on time. The guests at the event were happy, and many provided their compliments. However, the client had a handful of frivolous complaints, things like "not enough lemon in the water," and so on. Was it fair to leave one and two-star reviews on that basis? I certainly didn't think so.

Naturally, my client's first thought was to post a long rant he composed online, to show everyone just how wrong these customers were. Instead, I reminded him that we had to be professionals and remain polite. I explained that responding to complaints like these, even silly ones, shows that you are listening and open to improvement.

In the end, I had my client post his own explanation which was polite, factual, and to-the-point. In addition, we emailed his other current and recent customers asking them for their feedback. In just under a week, his business had a 4.5 star rating on Google and Yelp. The overwhelming positive feedback has drowned out the unreasonable complaints that were leveled in his direction. And the client has gotten into the habit of directing happy customers to these review sites by sending them links directly.

Problems with your online reputation can become opportunities for improvement — but only if you approach them with the right mindset and a plan to move forward.

Chapter 5: Growing a Healthy Online Reputation

Regardless of whether you started out with no online reputation, a small one, or even one with a few red flags, at some point you'll want to go beyond simply setting up profiles and responding to subpar reviews. It isn't enough to simply be visible on the Internet – you want potential customers, vendors, and employees to see good things about you and your business. That way, they'll come to you in a friendlier, more trusting frame of mind.

I covered some of the benefits of a positive online reputation in the opening chapter, and we'll explore the topic a little deeper towards the end of the book. Right now however, I just want to remind you that a positive online reputation isn't just about keeping new customers from being scared. It can also affect sales, negotiations, recruiting, and even your ability to form partnerships and get financing.

Why mention these benefits again now? Because growing your online reputation is an ongoing activity. It's something that takes a bit of work when you get started, and a little more perseverance after that. While there *is* a point where your online reputation will start to take on a life of its own, and generate its own momentum, that's usually something that happens after you've established a few good habits.

In this brief chapter, I'm going to show you what those good habits are. Let's look at some steps you can take to grow a healthy online reputation once you've established your profiles on the web…

A Good Online Reputation Starts Offline

I've already made this point a couple of different ways, and for a very good reason: if you get nothing else from this book, I hope you'll come away with the knowledge that your online reputation is important to your business, and that it's the direct extension of your business itself.

The companies with great reputations – the ones with thousands of social media fans and followers, and an endless stream of positive reviews – don't end up in that position by accident. They aren't just lucky. They are inevitably the ones who go above and beyond the call of duty when it comes to making buyers happy. They listen to their customers and respond to the feedback they get, regardless of whether it's positive or negative.

There are a lot of things in your company, and the economy at large, that you can't control. However, one thing you *can* always manage your attitude about is customer service. If you're focused on making sure that every transaction (or interaction) is a good one, that's going to come through when you're dealing with customers. They, in turn, will respond by saying good things about your business… even in situations that don't go as planned.

This isn't a new idea, but it's one that is often overlooked. The biggest opportunities to win customers and enhance your reputation are often found in the moments when it looks like the business is going to get away.

Let me share a quick illustrative example. A friend of mine decided to take a trip to the mountains in Colorado. He made his reservation well in advance, paying for a nice room at a luxury ski resort. Once he arrived with his family, however, there were several issues. The fireplace was out of order, the climate control was out of whack, and there was visible damage to some of the furniture.

My friend was understandably disappointed, and asked if his family could be relocated to another room. The resort manager informed him that the property looked to be "all booked up," but would follow up and see what she could do.

The story could have ended at this point, and my friend would have had a so-so vacation experience (complete with a so-so review online at the end of the trip). Instead, the resort manager got creative and relocated his family to an even bigger suite – one that had recently been remodeled – at a property next door. She apologized for the maintenance issues and provided them with a gift certificate to a local restaurant.

What do you think my friend's impression is of this resort now? What started out as a negative experience turned into an overwhelming positive one, to the point that he not only left a great review but has returned with his family several times since that first visit. Going the extra mile probably cost the hotel next to nothing. But, with a little bit of effort they were able to improve their reputation and win a customer for life.

What I really want to impress upon you is that your online reputation doesn't exist in a vacuum. It didn't drop out of the sky one day with no warning. Instead, it is likely to be the sum of the experiences customers have had with you and your business (difficult people and strange situations notwithstanding).

If you hire good employees, charge fair prices, and are transparent in the way you do business, having a positive online reputation is going to be a natural byproduct. On the other hand, if you come off as untrustworthy, you can't be surprised when the feedback you receive isn't all that great.

Highlight Customers and Positive Experiences

If often seems like building a great online reputation is largely a passive activity, where you do the best you can and hope for the right results. That's certainly the case more often than not. However, you can also be proactive in your approach. One of the ways to do this is by highlighting customers and positive experiences.

Most of us have seen a business website or Facebook company page where a "customer of the month" has been singled out. Usually, this person tells his or her story, along with some aspect of how the products or services being offered fit into their day-to-day lives.

Using those kinds of profiles is a great idea. For one thing, it lets buyers see that other people like themselves are benefiting from doing business with you (which increases your credibility). At the same time, it also creates a situation where others might want to reciprocate. That is, they may be so happy to be featured that they are willing to write reviews and testimonials on your behalf.

The same thing can happen in a more natural and organic way when you post about customer success stories, new partnerships, and other positive experiences of any kind. In fact, they don't necessarily have to be related to your business or industry at all.

One of the best ways to increase your online reputation is by participating in charitable events and drives. Unless the underlying cause is deeply controversial, being charitable shows others that you and your business are involved, and helping to develop the community at large.

In addition, many nonprofits like to sing the praises of their sponsors and volunteers. That could mean announcements, press releases, and mentions in marketing materials. Each of these helps to improve your online reputation (and bring visibility to your business) and a very positive way.

To be clear, I'm not suggesting that you should support charity, or say good things about the men and women who keep you in business, simply because it's good for your business. As a number of wise people have pointed out through history, doing a good deed is its own reward. But, while you're out there changing the world and making customers happier, don't be afraid to highlight your favorite causes and people. They might turn around to do the same for you, and then everyone wins.

Make Positive Reviews a Priority

I've already mentioned that there is a bit of luck involved in gaining positive reviews, and that will probably always be the case. Many customers, even deeply satisfied ones, simply won't take the time to write something nice, either because they don't realize how important it is, because they value their privacy too much, or for some other reason that you'll never find out.

If growing a strong online reputation is important to you, however, you should do what you can to create your own luck and convince some of those buyers who *could* be persuaded to leave you good feedback to do so.

There are two very easy ways to go about this. The first is to simply get things started with your best existing customers, as I've already mentioned. If you don't have much of an online reputation yet, or need to balance out a few negative reviews, starting with established business relationships is a good first step.

Just explain to them that you've come to realize how important online reviews are, and you'd love it if they could take just one or two minutes to say something positive about you and your company. If you've been good to work with, most of your close contacts will happily do so.

The second step is to simply let new buyers know that online reviews can make or break your business. Often, customers don't really realize how important their feedback is, and just how persuasive it can be to someone who's on the fence about a product, service, or company.

One of my vendors recently relayed the story of a vacation he took to the Pacific Coast in Mexico. One night, he decided that it would be great to have some fresh fish tacos. The only problem was that there were roughly two or three *dozen* restaurants serving fish tacos within walking distance of his hotel.

A quick look on TripAdvisor showed that one restaurant in particular – a smaller place, off the beaten path – had hundreds and hundreds of four and five star reviews. One diner after another swore that it was *the* place to go for this type of cuisine.

After a 10-minute walk, my vendor found out why. The meal was excellent, the seafood was fresh, and the prices were unbeatable. At the end of the dinner, along with the check, came a note:

Dear guest,

We hope you had a wonderful experience in our restaurant. If there was anything that was not up to your standards, or if you have any suggestions for improvement, we hope that you will share your thoughts and concerns with us before you leave.

If you were satisfied with your meal, we ask you to do us one small favor and take 60 seconds to share your thoughts on TripAdvisor. We know that you are busy enjoying your vacation, but as a small, family-owned establishment we don't have much money to spend on advertising. To compete with the larger restaurants in our area we rely on the kindness of happy customers like you to spread the word.

Thank you again for dining with us, we hope to see you again soon!

The note was signed in pen by the manager, who also made a point of introducing himself to each table at some point during the meal.

This is a business that gets the power of online reputation management, and the way it can overcome disadvantages of location, advertising, and brand recognition. It's also a perfect illustration of how you can ask your customers for a little help in getting the word out when they are already thinking good things about your business.

To be sure, there is such a thing as being *too* pushy when it comes to asking for online reviews. Pester customers too much, and they may decide to ignore you all together, or even write something that isn't exactly glowing just because you've hounded them into it.

Remember that and make online reviews a priority without going overboard. Know that some customers, even very happy ones, just aren't going to take the time. But by letting buyers know just how important their feedback is to you and the future of your business, you'll be pleasantly surprised at how many of them will be willing to post a few kind words on your behalf.

Should You Offer Compensation for Reviews?

One question that inevitably comes up in my keynote presentations and workshops is whether it's ethical, or even advisable, for business to pay for reviews. This is a nuanced subject, and so it requires an answer with a couple of different layers.

The first thing to know is that you should *never* hire any company that offers to post lots of false reviews on your behalf. These schemes don't work, and could permanently damage your business' reputation. On top of that, they could leave you liable for charges of fraud, false advertising, and lots of other nasty things.

Review sites monitor activity carefully. There are numerous ways they can spot attempts to game the system, including reviews that show up unexpectedly and in large quantities, feedback posted from faraway cities or foreign countries, several reviews coming from the same computer, and so on. At the first sign of trouble, they will suspend your account, remove all of your reviews, and possibly even add some note to your profile that suggests you've tried to engage in review fraud. None of that is going to help your online reputation.

The next step down would be having friends and relatives write reviews on your behalf. While this is a bit less likely to get you in hot water, it's still not a great idea. That's because these types of reviews are still technically "false," and could put your profiles at risk. Plus, savvy users might figure out that the reviews aren't genuine, which is a sure-fire way to trigger an onslaught of negative feedback. Once potential customers get the sense that you're trying to fool them, they'll be relentless with their abuse.

Finally, we come to the issue of encouraging reviews by offering compensation (for example, a free product or gift card to anyone who leaves a review for your business). Technically, this isn't illegal or disallowed, with the caveat that you have to make your offer available to *anyone* who leaves a review, regardless of whether it's positive or negative.

Recognizing the importance of online reviews, social media, and reputation management, the FTC has begun cracking down on unethical practices. One of their points of emphasis has been the idea that any paid reviews have to be labeled as such, and that compensation for reviews has to be provided regardless of the outcome. So, if you're giving away iPads to people who leave you testimonials, and one of your clients gives you a one-star review, they are getting an iPad just like everyone else.

On top of that, the best reviews are the ones written by customers who are satisfied and want to see you succeed, not the ones posted by price-conscious buyers who want to get something for free. Compensating for reviews might not get you in trouble, but it isn't the best way to enhance your online reputation, either.

Chapter Six: Going Deep With Advanced Online Reputation Improvement Strategies

---

If you have followed me through each of the chapters so far, then you already have a head start on your colleagues and competitors when it comes to online reputation management. In fact, you could probably stop reading now and have the tools you need to establish and grow the kind of profile that would help you attract the best customers and employees.

But that doesn't mean you should end your efforts there. In this chapter, I'm going to share with you some more advanced (and effective) online reputation management tactics you can use to give yourself a leg up.

Some might be redundant or unnecessary for your particular business. That's fine. Not everyone is in a super-competitive market, has lots of damage to repair in their past reviews, or has the resources available to devote to all of the tips listed below. However, most business owners will be able to manage at least a few of them, and putting any of these strategies to use can pay you back in a big way over the long run.

With that in mind, let's look at some of the ways you can keep your reputation growing and improving that go beyond the advice I've already given...

Check Your Social Media Privacy Settings

I made the point earlier that you should maintain separate personal and professional social media accounts. That won't mean much, however, if you don't change your privacy settings so that people who aren't in your circles or contact lists can't see your content.

An amazing number of individuals never bothered to change their privacy settings at all, meaning that anything they post to Facebook, Twitter, or any other social media account is open for the world to see. That's not always a good thing, even if you aren't a business owner or prominent community member. Take my advice and spend a few minutes it takes to adjust your settings now if you haven't already.

Also, remember that even with privacy safeguards in place, the things you post on social profiles can make their way into the public view… and in fact, if they are racier controversial enough, they probably will. Assume that there is a good chance anything you post, even privately, could be made public and act accordingly.

Emphasize Anything That Grows Your Reputation Locally

Although people can theoretically learn about your business from a computer, smart phone, or tablet anywhere in the world, most companies get the bulk of their business (and especially their best customers) from a local geographic area. This has always been true, but it's even more important in the age of local search engine optimization (Google and the other engines factor geography into search results) and social media.

How do you grow your reputation locally? That's easy: include your city or state name in updates to webpages, blog posts, and social profiles. Encourage customers to post their reviews on websites that apply to your neighborhood, and look for ways to engage the local press, as well as business directories that cover your city.

Get Attention From the Local and Business Press

One of the simplest ways to build your online reputation in a positive way, and help your business at the same time, is to get attention from the local and/or business press. And, getting coverage for yourself or your company is probably easier than you might think.

It's a little-known secret in the business world, but the editors of trade magazines, business newsletters, and even local dailies often have trouble filling their pages, especially during a slow news season. By sending out a press release, pitching a story, speaking at a public event, or just doing something noteworthy (like holding a contest on social media) you stand a good chance of getting them to take notice.

When reporters and bloggers are covering you, lots of good things happen. For one thing, it makes your business seem higher-profile and more credible. It also builds links back to your website, which helps you to maintain a strong search engine position.

Most importantly, though, being covered in the local press gets people talking about you and opens the door for *further* news stories and follow-ups in the future. So, if you have something to say, make sure the editors of publications in your area or industry hear about it.

Keep an Eye on Available Domain Names

If you're worried about people confusing you with another business – or worse, a competitor trying to snag customers who were looking for you online – then you might consider buying up domain names that are related to your name (personally), your company name, and anything related to your business or location.

That might sound like a big task, but there are number of places you can turn online to find available domain names that are close to yours (including common misspellings), and they can probably be purchased in bulk for as little as five dollars apiece. Best of all, it ensures that no one is going to put up a competitor's website on a domain that's very similar to the one you use.

Keep an Eye on Close Competitors

As a rule of thumb, it's better to worry about your own business than it is someone else's. And yet, one aspect of good online reputation management is knowing what "the guy down the street" is up to.

The obvious reason for this is because you want to protect yourself from those who don't have much of a moral compass. It's unfortunate, but review fraud, negative SEO, and fake complaints are all part of modern Internet marketing and reputation management. The chances that you'll be affected by these kinds of activities are low, but they aren't nonexistent. By keeping an eye on the competition, you can spot problems while they're on the horizon.

The less obvious reason to follow your competitors online is that they are likely to encounter the same kinds of problems with their reputation as you are with yours. There is an old riddle that goes like this: "If you wake up in the morning to discover that your closest competitor has gone out of business, is it good news or not?" Think about that one for a moment. Most business owners assume less competition and means more sales, but it *also* means that someone else couldn't make a viable business out of what you're doing.

The same thing applies to reputation management. If you see another business in your area or industry having lots of problems because of a certain type of customer or challenge, don't wait for it to start affecting you. Make a plan for combating the problem immediately. Otherwise, your reputation can be the next one to suffer.

Get Help Monitoring and Managing Your Online Reputation

I'm not going to spend a lot of time on this point, partly because this book is geared at helping you to manage your own online reputation, and partly because it seems self-serving to mention the availability of a service that I regularly provide (online reputation management). But I wouldn't be doing my job if I didn't at least provide a few thoughts in this area.

Usually, when a small business needs help with online reputation management, it's for one of two reasons: either they are trying to dig out of a terrible hole (caused by years of bad reviews or an unethical competitor), or because things have gotten so busy that they just can't manage social media activity updates on their own.

In either case, having a trained and experienced professional come in isn't the worst idea in the world. That's because an online reputation specialist doesn't just bring a specific set of skills to the table, but also a new perspective. He or she is likely to see things in a way that you haven't.

At the same time, it's also important to note that there are a lot of people out there calling themselves online reputation experts who have little knowledge or experience in the field. Maybe they know how to post a review to Yelp, or block someone on Facebook, but they don't understand the bigger picture and the way the different tools and techniques work together.

By reading this far into the book, you've armed yourself with enough knowledge to tell the difference, so don't pay money to someone who promises you the world but doesn't have the right credentials, or can't give you a specific plan that shows what they'll actually do to improve your online reputation.

Turn to the Legal System

Earlier, I mentioned that things like review fraud, fake reviews, and false accusations from customers are very rare, and they are. But, all of them do occur in the real world, and if you are targeted in one of these scams, it can have a very significant effect on your business… or even put you out of business altogether.

For that reason, it may be necessary – under very rare and unusual circumstances – for you to consult an online reputation management expert *and* a lawyer who can stop these activities from continuing, undo the damage, and possibly help you to seek compensation for the wrongs that have been done.

This is an extreme step, and one that I would only advise in very rare situations. Not only are lawyers expensive, but things like fraud can be difficult to prove on the Internet. So, proceed with caution if you're even thinking about going in this direction, but know that you do have some forms of recourse available to you if you're being harassed by another party with bad intentions.

Change Your Name, Brand, or Company

If pursuing legal action is extreme, then this is the online reputation management version of the "nuclear option." In most cases, it wouldn't make sense to make significant changes to a viable business just to shrug off a few bad reviews. However, there are times when it actually does make sense to blow the whole thing up and start over.

You see this at the Fortune 500 level from time to time, when a company is involved in a major accident, lawsuit, or scandal. Occasionally, the PR hit is so severe that there's nothing left to do but change the business name or chain the door shut altogether.

Very occasionally, you see the same kind of thing happen on a smaller scale with online reputation management. Perhaps a business has acquired *hundreds* of poor reviews over time, or the business owner has become reviled because of his or her outlandish personal statements. Maybe it's the case that a number of former employees have come out with some shocking behind-the-scenes FAQs.

The point, in each of these hypothetical instances, is that the business is no longer profitable (or won't be in the near future) because of the information that's out there for everyone to see. When that happens, there isn't much sense in putting the toothpaste back in the tube. All you can do is try to decide whether the image can be repaired, or if it makes more sense to pack up and call it a day on the venture in question.

Chapter 7: Setting Good Social Media Policies for Your Business

---

A huge portion of your online reputation is going to be determined by the way your employees interact with the public, and impressions shared and spread throughout social media are going to have a giant impact, as well. Bring those two ideas together, and it's not difficult to see how what you and your staff post to social media sites is going to go a long way towards shaping the way people feel about you and your company.

In many ways, that's going to be completely out of your control. That's just the nature of social networking. But by having smart, common-sense policies in place, you can help your employees to make smart decisions that enhance your online reputation and minimize the odds you'll find yourself having to explain an unfortunate tweet or post.

In this chapter, I'm going to share a few of the basics of social media policy for small businesses. Now that you know why you should have one, let's look at what it should include and how you put it in place...

Make Reputation Management a Part of Training

Odd as it might seem, many of the blunders you see small business owners and employees make online aren't committed by people wanting to be hurtful or destructive. Often, it's just the case that they really didn't know any better.

If you make social media a part of your new employee training, or something that you spend a little bit of time on once or twice a year, there's a good chance your staff will begin to appreciate how important your businesses online reputation is. Better yet, they'll understand how they fit into the picture, and what they can do to protect your company (not to mention their jobs).

There are a lot of things you could cover in basic social media training. Three very important topics might be when it is (and isn't) okay to access social media at work, what kinds of things can and can't be revealed about the company and its products or customers, and how employees can avoid violating intellectual property rights (which could lead to expensive fines and penalties for your company).

Covering topics like these wouldn't take much time, but can make all the difference when someone who works for you is about to make a very public or expensive mistake.

Decide Who Will Post To Your Company's Social Accounts, and When

As the business owner, you might well decide that you're the only one who will be authorized to post information to your company's social media profiles. But, as simple as that approach is, it's also a bit problematic. What happens if you're busy, or away on vacation? And, what kinds of opportunities could you be missing out on by not letting your employees use social media for things like customer service?

The best way to get around these issues is to decide up-front who has the green light to post to your company's social media profiles (or any associated accounts), and when they can do so. Putting these items into a written plan helps clear up confusion, divides responsibility in an easy-to-understand way, and makes it easier for you to keep a consistent online profile and reputation.

Create a Social Media Messaging Guide

Regardless of whom you're going to have posting to your accounts, it's a good idea to also have a written set of guidelines – even if it's just a single sheet of paper – that communicates what is and isn't acceptable, appropriate, or on-message when it comes to your company's social media messaging.

If you want to go more in-depth, you can also specify details like the length and timing of messages, what types of language you want to use, whether certain things should be capitalized or abbreviated, and so on. None of these might seem like a big deal, but they do all feed into the consistency of your overall brand and messaging.

At a minimum, though, your social media messaging guide should specify the personality of your business (whether you want to be serious, funny and lighthearted, etc.), what kinds of posts you want to see added, and what kinds of details are acceptable to share online.

Put Privacy at the Forefront

As social networking has become more and more ubiquitous, online privacy is gotten to be a bigger issue. For individuals, that means being careful what we share about ourselves and our friends; for businesses, it means considering privacy, and even legal liabilities, when we post to Facebook, Twitter, and other social platforms.

Make no mistake: we live in a day and age where you can be sued for putting information about customers, employees, and vendors online. That's particularly true if what you post is sensitive, damaging, or otherwise problematic.

Even putting the issues of liability aside though, holding tight to customer and employee privacy is just good business. You might think it's great that your favorite customer comes in every Tuesday to buy a doughnut and a large coffee, for example, but he might not want his spouse to know that he's not sticking to his diet, or for his employer to find out that's why he's taking so long on a service call. These are just hypothetical situations, but they illustrate an important fact, which is that we can't assume the people we work and deal with will be fine with us posting anything about them without their consent.

This doesn't mean that you can't ever share anything on your social accounts, of course — just that you should make sure that everyone on your team knows how important it is to get someone's consent before mentioning them or sharing personal details. Even things as innocuous as birthdays, promotions, or announcements can cause problems if they aren't handled the right way.

Set Employee Social Media Guidelines

Most of the issues concerning what is being posted by your company are fairly easy to avoid with a little bit of good training and direction. But, what about the things your employees are saying on social media away from the workplace on their own personal accounts?

This is where things get a little bit trickier. Court rulings in the last few years have made it clear that employers can't always dictate what their workers are able to post on social media. For instance, the National Labor Relations Board has made it clear that you can't prevent employees from airing legitimate workplace gripes on personal accounts. And yet, you can't have employees spreading false, personal, or confidential information, either.

To show you why this can be such an important and sticky issue, let me tell you the story of one of my clients, the owner of a small hair salon. This client had an employee who felt the need to share all the details of her day – including the hours she spent at work – on a personal Facebook account.

On the employee's Facebook page, the name of the salon wasn't ever mentioned. However, because of the location, pictures, etc., her place of employment would have been obvious to anyone reading her updates. Intentionally or not, this employee walked a very fine line. She never outright bashed the company she worked with, but she did complain repeatedly about the type of hair coloring product being used, the lack of free drinks and amenities for customers, and so on.

Had my client set up some form of social media policies, and had each new employee sign something saying they understood them and would adhere to them, she would have been able to put a stop to this daily activity (which she felt was affecting her ability to book new customers). But, because she hadn't, her only recourse was to attempt to take that step after the fact and hope she could convince this employee, and the others, that remaining positive and professional on Facebook would benefit all of them in the long run.

In the end, I directed my client to a website called *Social Media Governance* and advised her to not only develop written social media guidelines, but have them reviewed by an attorney. The moral of the story? Employees who pour their heart and soul out on social media every day aren't likely to care much about their employer's online reputation, so it's important to have these types of conversations with new staff when they're hired… not later when it's become a problem.

Check the Fine Print

It probably won't surprise you to know that the legal guidelines concerning social media in the workplace are not only new, but constantly changing. So, before you put any kind of written policy in place, it's not a bad idea to have a lawyer who specializes in this area look them over to ensure they won't leave you open to any claims later.

Better yet, if you tell such an attorney what you're looking for – and especially what you want to prevent – they may have a boilerplate version that you can use very inexpensively. Taking this step helps protect you from unnecessary problems later, especially if you need to approach an employee about his or her social activity, or even let them go because they have damaged your online reputation.

Whatever you do, take these written policies seriously, and be sure to have them reviewed at regular intervals (for instance, once every year). Legal standards are changing constantly, and what your employees post about you online can impact your business in a big way.

Social Media Policies: Supervise and Follow, But Don't Micromanage

In a lot of companies, it makes sense to have employees involved in social media, but it's also a good idea to protect yourself against them, their ideas, and their posts. This makes social media policies a double-edged sword. On the one hand, you definitely want to provide training and guidance, but on the other hand you shouldn't (and legally can't) micro-manage your staff, especially when it comes to their personal accounts.

So direct them towards crafting social media posts that are appropriate for your business, and follow their activities online in a casual way, if you can. But don't obsess over every update or tweet, and refer back to your written policies if you see a problem. That's not always a perfect solution, but it's probably the best approach you can use in the digital age.

Chapter 8: Common Online Reputation Management Mistakes

While we've looked at many of the best practices around online reputation management already, it might also be helpful to stop and take a look at what we might call the *not so best practices*. These are the common online reputation management mistakes that are so easy to make, that you might find yourself slipping into them unintentionally.

Some of the blunders below have already been covered, and a few should barely need mentioning at all. To make sure we've covered our bases, we'll begin with the ones that are the simplest and most innocuous, and end up with the worst of the worst.

Here are a handful of things you should definitely *not* be doing online…

Failing to Establish an Online Presence

Just because you have a website doesn't mean it's easy for customers, vendors, and potential employees to find you. It's important to ensure that you're visible – and that people who want to reach you can do so *in a way that's convenient to them* – by establishing profiles on industry websites and major social media platforms.

Don't just assume that having a website is enough. Sometimes, customers will want, or even *need*, to look for you elsewhere. Let's look at a quick, real-world example that shows why.

I'm a big fan of the television show *Shark Tank*. In fact, I actually know someone who once made an appearance on the program.

If you aren't familiar with it, the premise is simple: entrepreneurs come up before a panel of billionaire investors to pitch their ideas. If the presentation is successful, the investors may buy a stake of the business and offer their expertise; if not, the entrepreneurs walk away with nothing more than a bit of feedback. It's the perfect mixture of business insight and reality TV.

Perhaps it's because of the work I do on a daily basis, or it might just be because I'm curious, but I tend to Google the names of the companies that are being presented as the show unfolds and look a bit closer. Apparently, I'm not the only one. I know this because my friend (who was on the show but didn't leave with the deal) saw traffic to his website spike during his segment.

Unfortunately, this friend was using cheap web hosting, and his server couldn't handle the volume. His website actually crashed, and was offline for days afterward! Wasting an appearance on national television might have been disastrous, from a marketing perspective, had his Facebook page not been online and updated.

However, as soon as his website went offline, he started receiving new inquiries via the company's Facebook page. Although he probably still lost money from having a website that was "out of order," he did at least make some new contacts that he could follow up with later.

Even if his website hadn't failed, the Facebook page would have been a good alternative for new fans and interested potential customers who wanted to get in touch with him through medium they already use every day. The fact that his website *did* go down just illustrates that it's always good to have an online presence that's bigger than your company domain.

Leaving Your Accounts and Profiles for Dead

When your social media accounts and business profiles are incomplete, or rarely updated, it sends a signal to potential customers that your business either isn't currently in operation, or can't keep up with details. Either way, you aren't exactly inviting feedback, positive reviews, or any kind of attention at all when you leave your accounts and profiles unattended. Make a plan to log-in at least once a week to see what's going on and add a few new thoughts.

Putting the Wrong Person in Charge of Your Social Media Accounts

In small businesses, it isn't unusual to find that an intern or part-time employee is essentially dictating social media strategy for everyone. Usually, the rationale goes something like: "They are already using Twitter all day anyway, so why not?" That might be convenient, but it isn't smart. Remember that everything posted online in your name can help or hurt your reputation. Choose someone you can trust to make good decisions, and then make sure you're still involved in the process, even if it's just with a bit of occasional oversight.

Hardly a week goes by when we don't hear about social media "fails" that result from someone's carelessness or ignorance about the way social media works. I'll give you just a couple of examples I've witnessed myself...

Here is an infamous tweet from Chrysler: *I find it ironic that Detroit is known as the #motorcity and yet no one here knows how to f*&%ing drive!*

That's not great, but at least it wasn't as bad as a famous KitchenAid's tweet, which joked about the death of President Obama's grandmother. The company quickly issued a statement pointing out that the message was an obvious mistake on the part of an individual employee, but the blunder was quickly covered by the national media and still shows up as a prominent search result when you investigate the company on Google.

Once something that's harmful to your reputation has been posted or tweeted online, you can't get it back. You might be able to delete the message from your feed, but it will still be on the Internet for all to see. Knowing that, it's crucial that you restrict access to your social accounts to those who have the good taste to use them appropriately.

Ignoring Negative Reviews and Online Feedback

A lot of business owners and managers like to treat negative reviews as if they don't exist, or they never happened. That's a big mistake. For one thing, it leaves a dissatisfied customer in a dissatisfied state, which means you're probably not going to get any further business from them in the future. Even worse, it leaves a big red flag on the Internet for other people to find and notice. That's never going to be good for sales, so make sure you resolve the problem and get a revised review from the complaining customer if it's at all possible.

Remember earlier, when I told you about the CPA firm in Chicago with the not-so-nice employees? Stop and think for a moment what might have happened if he had ignored the poor feedback his firm and gotten. Had he continued to let his problem employee treat customers in an unprofessional way, it might have caused other clients to leave and prevented him from finding new ones... it might have even put him out of business altogether.

Deciding not to ignore negative reviews doesn't necessarily mean you're always going to apologize, either. You can't please everyone, and telling your side of the story at least gives potential customers another perspective to consider.

Some people who complain about your business are going to be flat-out wrong. In addition to my web design and online reputation consulting business, I also run a retail computer store. I once had a customer who left a poor review on our Facebook page stating that we didn't stand behind our products. In particular, his issue was that we wouldn't accept a power cord that had been broken.

What he neglected to mention in his review, of course, was that the cord was broken because his dog had chewed it in half. When he first brought into the store, I offered to replace it at cost, but declined to give him a new part for free.

I could have let that online review go, but it was important to me that other customers know what had happened. So, I responded online with a note that said, in effect: "I'm sorry you felt disappointed by the way we dealt with your situation. We take satisfaction very seriously, but it was obvious that your dog had chewed the power cord for your computer in half. I'm glad your dog is all right, and am still willing to replace your cord at cost. Of course, had there been an issue with the part we sold you I would have gladly replaced it or refunded your money on the spot."

After a couple of hours, other customers were commenting on the original review, noting that it was unfair to expect my company to pay for a power cord that had become a chew toy. Simply taking five minutes out of my day to respond was enough to mitigate the damage.

Before long, the customer took the review down from our Facebook page on his own. And a couple of days later, he showed up at the store to purchase a replacement cable. (And in case you're wondering, yes, I still sold it to him at cost...)

Forgetting to Ask Customers for Reviews

Just as you can't ignore bad reviews, it's hard for your business to grow and succeed in the digital age without having lots of positive feedback. When you leave things to chance, you're only likely to get reviews from people who are extremely impressed (and remember about it later), those who are dissatisfied enough to speak up, and the small handful of individuals who regularly leave reviews for everything. Make a habit of asking buyers to say good things about you online and your online reputation will grow steadily over time.

Using Your Profiles to Brag and Boast

One of the interesting side effects that's come with the growth of the Internet and social media is that lots of people want to be wealthy superstar celebrities, or at least appear to be that way. But going too far in an effort to make yourself seem successful can easily backfire in a big way.

Years ago, I had a favorite business author whose work really impressed me. I read all of his books, followed his blog, and even shared his social updates to my own contacts on a regular basis. If you were one of my clients, or someone who was following me on Facebook or Twitter, you were bound to see his quotes (attributed, of course) in my own updates on a regular basis.

During this time, I happened to be one of his first Facebook followers. I actually love the fact that he promoted his new books, recordings, and other products, since it meant I didn't have to visit his website to find out what to buy. It's hard to imagine anyone who might have been a more loyal (and profitable) customer than I was at that point.

After a while, though, his posts steered away from the regular staples of time management, negotiation, and other business tips, and focused more and more on his Bentley, his trophy wife (his words), and the other trappings of his success. One long rant even included details of an interaction where he interrogated a bank teller only to realize that he had deposited his insanely-large royalty check at another bank. LOL, right?

His "my great life" theme was wearing thin on me. The breaking point came, though, when the response to any question from a fan was a condescending remark or a reminder that he charged $1000 per hour for consulting. I realized that I was tired of hearing so much about life in the millionaires club, that he wasn't interested in helping or educating his fans anymore, and that his profile was a waste of time. In just a few minutes, I had unfollowed his page, unfriended him, and sold the autographed copy of his book that I owned.

There's nothing wrong with being yourself and enjoying your triumphs — but think about the messages you're sending to your followers when you post. You might want the world to think that you're an overnight success, but remember that they can cut you out of their lives in just a few seconds.

Not Having a Written Social Media Policy

As I mentioned in the last chapter, it's important for every organization of any size to have a written social media policy, even if it's a simple one-page document that outlines what employees can do to protect you from liability involving copyright, privacy, or intellectual property claims.

If you're not talking to your staff about social media, then you can't really complain when they start bashing your business, sharing details of sensitive customer interactions, or letting loose information about your private life and/or profitability. Do yourself a favor and put some written guidelines in place that make it easy for those on your team to know how they should be behaving on the Internet, especially when they are representing you and your company.

Being Inflammatory

It's worth mentioning again that pushing too hard to share your own views on politics, religion, sports, or anything else can cost you in a big way. Numerous surveys have shown that social media followers are annoyed by online blowhards who pick fights, and that customers can and do decide to take their business elsewhere when they get the sense that an owner personality is more interested in their own agenda then building a business.

Note that this can happen even when others agree with what you have to say. Even if someone agrees with your philosophy or viewpoint, they might get sick of hearing about it when they are trying to conduct business. Or they might be worried what their association with you could say to other professional contacts in their own networks.

If you are constantly touching on hot topics using your business profiles, then you're probably playing with fire.

Letting the Internet Run Amok

Earlier, I advised you to look for ways to let fans and customers generate content and ideas on your behalf. Not only is that a convenient and inexpensive way to grow your online reputation, but you'll often be surprised at the creativity others will show.

There's a difference, though, between getting customers and supporters in on the act and letting the Internet run amok. To understand why, we have to remember that the Internet is a *thing*, but it's also a *group*. Or at least it can be a group, metaphorically-speaking. And usually, when we discuss "the Internet" as a group, it's not in a good way.

This is something so basic that we all understand it. Just look through the comments on a YouTube video, for example, to see how harsh and unrelenting people can be. Even clips of children and pets will attract some level of abuse from disaffected individuals who have nothing else to do with their time. Should we be surprised, then, that the same individuals will take their aim at a company (even a well-known one) if given the chance?

In the past few years, both McDonald's, Chick-fil-A, and Starbucks have committed huge online reputation blunders by asking people to contribute to campaigns that were, in hindsight, always going to fail (Google either these companies and "social media fail" if you aren't familiar with what I'm talking about). So, too, have a number of celebrities and worldwide brands.

Possibly the worst and most prominent example of this phenomenon, though, came from the formally-beloved entertainer Bill Cosby. At a time when public opinion about the comedian was shifting, due to numerous allegations of sexual assault raised by alleged victims that spanned the course of decades, his PR team decided to turn to social media as a way to influence public opinion.

I watched horrified when, in an effort to remind the country of why they had loved Cosby in the past, his social media manager asked followers to create their own Bill Cosby memes. He even provided the photos for them to get started with.

Now, for those of you who don't know already, a meme is a picture with a fun caption that can be shared quickly and easily across social media accounts. They often spread like wildfire, to the point that you've probably seen dozens of them already today.

In any case, this campaign opened up the wrath of the Internet in an almost unprecedented way. While there were a few fun and innocent submissions, the vast majority ended up with his face being attached to terrible jokes about drugs and rape. None of it was funny, and it was the polar opposite of what you'd consider "good online reputation management."

Not surprisingly, the staff pulled the meme project for Mr. Cosby's website within a few hours, but the damage had already been done. Literally thousands of offensive memes with the comedian's picture were being shared across social networks around the world.

The lesson here is simple: never, *never* turn your brand and identity over to the Internet. At best, you'll see people having a bit of harmless fun with your image or message. At worse, you'll discover the darker side to humanity that comes out when disturbed individuals have the option of hiding behind anonymity and their First Amendment rights. Things like slander and plagiarism are just the tip of the iceberg in these situations, so why open yourself up to them?

Lashing Out

There is a quote that's been around forever, and I'll give you a cleaned up version of it here: "When you wrestle with the pig, you both end up dirty and smelling like poop."

That's a good axiom to remember when you're tempted to lash out at someone who has given you a bad review online. No matter how scathing the feedback, or how unjustified you feel it is, remember that it's your job as a marketer to stay upbeat and positive. The customer may not always be right, but they are still the customer.

Time after time, I have seen business owners lash out at followers, attack reviewers, and try to discredit those who don't agree with them. There hasn't been a single one of these situations where I have seen the business come out ahead.

If you do feel tempted to direct your anger at someone for what they've said or posted, online or off, remember two things. First, that it isn't going to help, and in fact is probably going to cause them to double down on their position (and bring a lot of other people over to their side if it seems like you are overreacting). And second, that it probably wasn't personal.

As I've already pointed out, the anonymous nature of Internet posting makes some people express opinions more strongly than they would have otherwise. Everyday people start to think they are armchair comedians or reviewers. Often, by apologizing and responding rationally, you'll remind them that they aren't experts, and that you are a real person, too. In other words, it might cause them to reconsider and take back a negative review that was over-the-top.

Either way, know that lashing out never helps you or your online reputation. Take a deep breath, calm down, and then respond using the techniques I've already outlined in this book.

Taking Shortcuts

There aren't any shortcuts to building good word-of-mouth advertising off-line, which is why there aren't any shortcuts (or least not ones that work) to building a strong online reputation, either.

That doesn't mean there's any shortage of companies or vendors out there willing to sell you digital snake oil. Thousands of fans and followers, hundreds of great reviews, and a flood of new businesses are all there – or so they promise – so long as you're willing to fork over just a bit of your marketing budget. In reality, what you'll get are cheap reviews that will probably be removed (if they don't get you banned altogether), Facebook followers that are obviously robotic, and a permanent blow to the credibility of your business.

Building a strong online reputation can be a slow, painstaking process, but it's well worth the time and effort. When you do things right, every new post or review is a spark that can attract others, and ultimately help your bottom line. When you look for shortcuts, you end up wasting time and money while digging a hole that you might never get out of.

Slinging Mud

In the same way that you shouldn't look to take shortcuts to promote your own business, you shouldn't even *think* about posting fake negative reviews (or using similarly slimy tactics) to harm any of your competitors, either. For the same reasons I gave a moment ago, these tricks are generally ineffective. When they are directed at someone else, though, they have the added burden of being illegal and unethical. Take the low road, and you could end up facing such huge fines that you have to close your doors forever.

It's never worth it to start slinging mud at a competitor in an attempt to get ahead. If you suspect that someone else is doing it to you, investigate and take the appropriate legal action. Don't be drawn into that kind of fight, though, because there isn't really any way to win.

Chapter 9: Your Personal Online Reputation

To this point, we've looked at things you can do to grow and enhance the online reputation of your business. But what about your personal reputation? While you might think it doesn't matter what others say about you as a person, so long as they respect you as a professional, that's not necessarily the case. In fact, your personal and business reputations are connected in more ways than you probably realize.

The biggest reason to pay attention to your personal online reputation is that, as an entrepreneur, your reputation can strongly affect your business (in the minds of many prospects, you *are* the company). If people don't like, trust, or respect you, they are going to be wary of working with you.

Another reason is that having a strong reputation for yourself can open a lot of doors that go above and beyond your day-to-day business activities. I work with a lot of organizations as a web designer, for example, but also frequently give presentations on reputation management, small business Internet marketing, and other related topics. When attendees and meeting planners search for information about these sessions, they don't just visit my company website; they also look up my personal social accounts. Even if you don't have those kinds of ambitions now, you may in the future.

You should also consider the possibility that your needs and priorities might change at some point in the future. It's not unusual for business owners to become speakers, authors, and volunteers. In the same way, some tire of the stresses of running a business and return to the world of traditional employment at some point or another. If that ever happens to you, you'll want an online reputation that tells employers you are someone they should consider hiring.

The point that I want you to walk away with here is that your online reputation as an individual is just as important as the one you maintain for your business, if not more so, in the long run. With that in mind, let's take a look at what you can do to protect yours…

Maintain a Wall Between Your Personal and Business Profiles

Unless you have the kind of business (like a one-on-one consulting practice) where you literally are the company, you should try to maintain separate profiles on all the social media websites you use. In fact, even if you *do* have that kind of business, it's something you might want to consider anyway.

This is partly to keep personal details and opinions away from your business accounts – something I have probably mentioned often enough at this point to avoid dwelling on here. It's also for your own privacy, however. The more closely you are related to your business, the more likely it is that your name is being used in all kinds of marketing and promotion. Even if it's not intentional, that kind of activity is going to lead to others getting a bigger glimpse into your personal and private life than you might want.

The obvious and stereotypical stories here would be the woman who finds herself being stalked by a client who found personal details online, or the business owner who is scammed by a con artist who has researched them via social media. These types of situations might be rare and extreme, but they illustrate an important point: that you should be separate from your business, and only invite people you know into your personal social circles.

Maintain separate profiles for yourself and your company, and use privacy controls to stop your personal thoughts and details from being shared with the world. Your customers and associates don't need to know everything about your life, and you probably don't want them to, anyway.

Claim Your Own Name and Domains

In the same way that every company should own the domain names associated with the name of the business, its products, and any major branding points, it's also a good idea for individuals to register domains that match their names if they happen to be available. Even if you never decide to actually use them, owning them means you can stop others from posting offensive material that might be mistakenly attributed to you.

Going a step further, you can look for usernames on social media websites that match up to your real name, or at least make sure that your profiles are differentiated from others with similar names and locations. Part of good personal reputation management is just playing defense, and having control of your own name online is a good first step.

In the digital age, your domain name *is* your identity, and should be protected as such. For an easy illustration of the way this works, take a look at what happens to candidates during election years. Every cycle, there are some who don't own their own named domains, and as a consequence can't control the content that's placed there.

In the worst instances, these domains are purchased by competitors. At the time of this writing, Carly Fiorina (former CEO of Hewlett-Packard) is running for president. However, she failed to register CarlyFiorina.com. It would be bad enough if that domain were being used by another person with the same name. As it is, however, someone is using that space to put up a website that shows frowning faces – referencing the 30,000+ people she laid off while at the helm of HP.

Because her name predictably generates lots of Google searches, and an exact domain match comes up very early in the search rankings, this is one of the first things voters see when they go online to learn more about her. As you can imagine, it's not a great first impression.

Even if you aren't worried about running for office, having your name domain could be helpful. For instance, I purchased domains for both of my children. Someday they might want to use them to display portfolios that will help them get in college, or work as self-employed professionals. At the very least, if someone does a quick search for their names, they will be able to have a bit of control over the results.

That's not a small issue. I know of a comedian who jokes about having the same name as a serial killer. Even though he makes light of it, imagine how awful that would be… especially if you work in the public space, as he does, or if you were trying to get a job or impress a date.

Just this morning, I was looking up a phone number for my veterinarian. I typed his name and "animal" into a Google search, and got a few results about an animal abuser that shares his same name. Obviously, I knew these results weren't referencing him, but would others? And if a potential customer for his veterinary business couldn't tell the difference immediately, how likely would they be to call?

The bottom line is this: own your domain! If you haven't purchased yours already, do it *now*. Having your named domain is a great way to keep it safe and avoid confusion.

Want to do it right now before you forget? There is a link titled "secure your domain name" at (where else?) www.TammyFinch.com.

Clean up Red Flags One at a Time

It's ironic, but for as often as I get phone calls about bad reviews and other potentially damaging items to a company's online reputation, I almost never hear from individuals who worry about what they've posted online (or what's been posted about them). And yet, these types of details are just as easy to find, and potentially more damaging.

I've already laid out the case for protecting your privacy, so I won't go into that in further length.

However, I should note that old posts, and especially photos where you've been tagged, can come back to haunt you. You might think that any "incriminating evidence" about you has been buried in the past, but what happens when you're trying to close a multimillion dollar financing deal and the bank manager comes across a few "party pics" from five years ago? Or, when you're trying to win a big customer and they come across your drunken rant on YouTube?

Even if they don't ruin your chances of taking advantage of these opportunities, they certainly aren't going to help. And worse yet, a lot of the biggest red flags to be found in an individual's online reputation weren't even posted by the individual themselves, but added by friends or associates.

Luckily, cleaning up your personal online reputation is usually a pretty quick and painless process. First, you follow the steps that I outlined earlier in this book to discover what has been posted, both by yourself and others – including items you might have forgotten about years ago. Then, you go about changing or removing them one at a time.

The beauty of this system is that, in most cases, a simple email or request will do the trick. Unlike business and product review sites, which operate on the principle of providing useful feedback, most social media outlets are voluntary, and most people won't post something for the purpose of making us look bad or to hurt our careers. So, you can usually get something you don't want to see online removed within a matter of hours or days.

Depending on how extensive and "colorful" your past has been, it might make sense to approach things one at a time, over a course of days or weeks, keeping track of different items on a spreadsheet. It can be painstaking work, especially if you were previously the kind of person who posted *everything* to social media, but you'll probably see results faster than you might imagine.

Keep the Right Company

If you are a parent, your child probably has friends you approve of, as well as a few that you worry about. In our minds, we reflexively tend to think of "good kids" and "bad kids," and want our offspring to be associated with the one group and not the other.

This isn't just our overprotective selves worrying about the worst – as we all know, you tend to take on bits of the personality, habits, and attitudes of those around you. This notion is so dependable that psychologists claim most of us amount to a rough amalgamation of the five or ten closest people in our lives.

In terms of online reputation management, it isn't just that we are influenced by those we "hang out" with, even virtually, but that others tend to judge us by the company we keep. If we are associated with top professionals in our field, or even the best and brightest in other fields, people tend to assume that we fall into the same category. On the other hand, if our contact list and followers are filled with individuals making inappropriate jokes and trying to pass off spam links on a regular basis, that will likely be taken as a cue that we can't be trusted, either.

I'm not suggesting that you turn your entire life over and surrender decades-old relationships just for the sake of online reputation management. But, you should know that adding contacts who are at the top, or on their way up, is going to be much better for your profile (not to mention your personal outlook on life) than spending your online time with people who are negative and/or suspicious.

Making the right impression is easier when you keep the right company.

Stay Involved and Be Positive

We have already looked at the way empty and stagnant profiles make a business look like it's going out of business. The same thing applies, to a lesser degree, to your own social accounts and online profiles.

When you haven't posted anything for a long time, or followed up with messages and requests, it makes you seem like you either don't care about others or can't manage to stay on top of your life. There's no rule that says you have to sit on your social accounts constantly, but logging in for a few minutes every week – even if it's just to tell your contacts that you've been too busy to trade stories with them – is a great way to stay involved and show others what you've been up to. When you do have the time, adding a few thoughts, updates, or pictures can go a long way towards making yourself more known.

Just as with your business accounts, you should take care to keep a positive and professional tone whenever possible. You certainly don't have to be a robot, or respond to bad news with a false sense of upbeat cheerfulness, but neither should you constantly dwell on things that are negative or unfortunate.

Positive, cheerful people have a naturally attractive quality about them. If you want your personal online reputation to grow and improve, try to be known as someone who can see the brighter side, or at least the lighter side, of life and not a person who's always down in the dumps.

An Example of Personal Reputation Management Done Right

In the same way that establishing a great online reputation for your business can lead to more sales and a healthier bottom line, improving your personal reputation can pay big dividends, too. To give a quick example of how that works, let me tell you about the experiences of a friend who used her online reputation to transition to a whole new life.

When I first met her, she was in the process of moving to Central Illinois – and starting a new life – while coming from a much larger city on the East Coast. Although she had been successful as a marketing professional in the urban areas she was moving from, she had decided to make some life changes and relocate to a town where she didn't have any contacts at all.

As a first step, this enterprising young woman started following many of the more prominent marketing agencies in the area as a way to get familiar with the companies and their key contacts. While she was sure to keep an eye out for any new job postings, as most people searching for employment would, she also made a point of reading their posts and occasionally commenting on them.

Even though her responses were casual (and not focused on her job search), a funny thing began to happen: her name became familiar to the executives who were sharing ideas on Facebook, Twitter, and LinkedIn. Over the course of a few short months, she developed an "in" with the higher-ups at a handful of leading firms. Eventually, when she did send along her resume, they took notice and put her name at the top of the pile.

You can guess what happened next: my friend got a job at the firm she considered to be her first choice employer in the area. She didn't even have to apply for an opening; they created a special position for her that went from a part-time to a full-time opportunity very quickly.

My friend followed all the textbooks steps any person or business should if they want to generate new opportunities: she created complete profiles and used them actively. She made the right contacts, remained positive and professional, and looked for ways to share what she knew, rather than simply going into sales mode from the outset. And most of all, she stayed patient until the right chance came along.

Online reputation management is a powerful thing. Get it right, and it can open doors that you didn't even know were right in front of you.

Chapter 10: Some Parting Thoughts on Reputation Management

Finally, we've reached the end! If you've been following along, you know what your online reputation is, why it's so valuable, and which steps you need to take to both improve the impressions that new customers get about your business and establish a stronger identity going forward.

While we certainly could end things there, I'd like to leave you with a few parting thoughts on reputation management, including some final tips and a few words of encouragement...

Improving Your Reputation Takes Time

The Internet has trained all of us to be impatient. When we click a button, we want to see new information or content displayed *right away*. If we make a purchase online, we want the item to be in-stock and available for overnight delivery.

Some psychologists have suggested that the lightning-quick nature of the digital world has made us all more impatient. It's hard to dispute that notion when you see how frustrated people get over a little bit of traffic, or watch what happens when the Wi-Fi goes out at a coffee shop.

I bring that point up now because many business owners assume that cleaning up a poor online reputation, or building a better one, is something that can be accomplished in a matter of hours or days. While a lot of the first steps can be accomplished in that timeframe, the reality is that it's still going to take a while for search engines, social media followers, and customer impressions to catch up.

Remember what I've said all along: your online reputation is just your company's word-of-mouth, but expressed online. While you might be able to get someone to amend a bad review or give you some positive feedback through Twitter, there is still going to be a delay before Google finds that new information and changes its search results. And, more to the point, there is going to be a lag time in which people who have seen the old reviews (or haven't ever heard of your company at all) get a chance to "catch up" with your new reputation.

Don't get me wrong: by following the steps outlined in the previous chapters, you can start seeing better results – in your business and your own career – almost overnight. But, don't expect that all of the work is going to be done instantly, or that people are suddenly going to start saying the things you want them to in the blink of an eye.

Improving your reputation takes time, and it takes effort. It is well worth the work and the weight, but expecting that things will change instantly is often going to set you up for disappointment.

Reputation Management is Always Changing

I wish I could promise you that this short book would represent the last thing you'll ever have to read about online reputation management. But while it's a great introductory guide to the subject and should tell you everything you need to know about protecting your image online *now*, the fact of the matter is that this is a new subject, and one that's bound to keep changing for years to come.

To understand why, you only have to look at the growth of the Internet, and particularly social media websites, over the last decade or so. Once upon a time, MySpace was essentially the main hub for social activity; now it's just an afterthought in the discussion. At the time of this writing, Google + has come out of nowhere, gained almost 1 billion users, and seems to be on the verge of disappearing altogether (possibly to return in some new form in the near future).

I can't tell you what the next frontier will be in online reputation management. No one can.

Knowing that, your job isn't to learn about reputation management once and forget about it, but to remember the main principles I've given you – and particularly the notion that what others are saying about you and your company online affects your ability to attract customers, employees, and vendors – and then apply them to a changing digital world.

To be sure, there will be other resources, including my own blog posts and future updates to this book. However, nothing you can read on the subject will ever be completely forward-thinking, if only because the world of business is forever changing in the digital age. Just remember that your online reputation has the potential to be an incredibly valuable asset. Grow it, protect it, and look out for shifts in the future.

Good Reputation Management is a Positive Feedback Loop

One of the most fascinating things about human nature, and the world at large, is that so many processes tend to take on an accelerating nature. For example, you push a boulder down the hill, and it doesn't just keep rolling along, but picks up speed until it's practically flying. A meme shows up on a social media site and goes from a thousand views to 1 million in under two hours. A small business doubles its advertising budget and sees a 1000% sales bump.

In science, these kinds of phenomenon are called "positive feedback loops." They occur when a mechanism or reaction takes on a life of its own. These kinds of situations are extremely common when human psychology is involved.

As you might have suspected, online reputation management works exactly in this way. To have one or two positive reviews is a good thing and speaks volumes about your company and its products or services. Get two dozen great reviews, though, and you'll notice that new buyers will immediately start sharing their own thoughts, as well. At a certain point, your business becomes so popular that other people *expect* that they are going to like you, and they'll want to share the news with someone else.

None of that can or will occur, however, unless you get the ball rolling. There are companies that get fortunate and see their reputations grow all on their own, but those instances are rare. And, more often than not, they revolve around "fun" products that are marketed and sold to young people who tend to share their opinions about everything.

If you aren't in that kind of business – or, if you are and you just want to take more control of your company's future – then you are going to have to be the one to push the boulder. It's going to take some effort at first, and you might feel like you're getting nowhere even while you're straining the hardest. In the beginning, there might be little movement at all.

But, if you can stick with it and keep pushing, the process of online reputation management will kick in and start to move on its own momentum. Then, instead of pushing with all of your might, all you have to do is sit back, monitor its progress, and enjoy the rewards.

The practices outlined in this book work. I know, because I've seen them used to profitable effect dozens and dozens of times. What's more, I can promise you that if you do the hard work needed to improve your company's reputation, it will help you in numerous different ways.

Never forget that we live in a world where people research everything. They want to make smart decisions with their money, their time, and their careers. If Google and its many cousins on search and social media are constantly saying good things about your business, you're going to get more customers, better employees, and stronger relationships. On the other hand, if no one can find out anything about you – or what they see is largely negative – then you're always going to be fighting an uphill battle against public opinion.

Online reputation management isn't expensive, difficult, or time-consuming. But, if you don't pay attention to it, you're going to be at the mercy of luck. Isn't it time you start doing what you can to ensure that your name, and your business, are associated with the right kinds of impressions? And what will it mean for the future of your company when they are?

Good luck! I look forward to reading great things about you and your business.